To my parents, who first connected me to the internet; to all the friends
I made online; and to everyone who makes the internet.

C.S.

To the internet, for accompanying me through all these years.
Thanks for the teachings, entertainment and somewhat colourful content.

T.P.

A TEMPLAR BOOK

First published in the UK in 2026 by Templar Books,
an imprint of Bonnier Books UK
5th Floor, HYLO, 105 Bunhill Row, London, EC1Y 8LZ
The authorised representative in the EEA is Bonnier Books UK (Ireland) Limited.
Registered office address:
Floor 3, Block 3, Miesian Plaza, Dublin 2, D02 Y754, Ireland
compliance@bonnierbooks.ie
www.bonnierbooks.co.uk

Text copyright © 2026 by Craig Steele
Illustration copyright © 2026 by Terri Po
Design copyright © 2026 by Templar Books

1 3 5 7 9 10 8 6 4 2

All rights reserved

ISBN 978-1-80078-798-8

Edited by Rachael Roberts
Designed by Ceri Woods
Production by Neil Randles

Printed in China

FROM AI TO WI-FI
HOW THE INTERNET WORKS

Written by
CRAIG STEELE

Illustrated by
TERRI PO

templar
books

CONTENTS

- WELCOME TO THE INTERNET 4
- INTERNET HISTORY 6
- WHAT IS THE INTERNET? 8
- AI AND THE INTERNET 9
- THE INFRASTRUCTURE OF THE INTERNET 10
- HOW DATA IS SENT ACROSS THE INTERNET .. 12
- THE PEOPLE WHO KEEP US CONNECTED 14
- WHO MAKES THE INTERNET? 16
- PROGRAMMING LANGUAGES 20
- OPEN SOURCE TECHNOLOGY 22
- HOW THE INTERNET CHANGED:
  - SHOPPING 24
  - THE WAY WE LEARN 26
  - VIDEO GAMES 28
  - THE MUSIC INDUSTRY 30
- USER-GENERATED CONTENT 32
- HOW CREATORS MAKE MONEY 34
- WHO CONTROLS THE INTERNET? 36
- HOW FAIR IS THE INTERNET? 38
- CYBERCRIME ON THE INTERNET 40
- ENCRYPTION 42
- PROTECTING YOUR PERSONAL DATA 44
- SOLVING BIG PROBLEMS 46
- HOW THE INTERNET CHANGES LIVES 48
- HOW THE INTERNET CAN HARM US 50
- HOW THE INTERNET IMPACTS THE ENVIRONMENT 52
- CARING FOR THE INTERNET 54
- THE FUTURE OF THE INTERNET 56
- WHAT'S YOUR INTERNET PERSONA? 58
- SIGN OFF 60
- GLOSSARY 62

WELCOME TO THE INTERNET

Have you ever been told off for spending too much time online? That was me when I was your age. I was curious and eager to learn. So, you can imagine how amazed I was when I discovered the internet – a place where it seemed the answers to all my questions were just a click away.

I remember the squeals, beeps, chirps and electronic buzzes my 90s modem made when connecting to the internet. Back in those days, internet connections at home were shared with the telephone line. If my Mum made a phone call, it would disconnect me!

I remember creating my first website. It was a blog where I wrote about my favourite TV shows. Now, you'd probably laugh at how it looked, but I was so proud to share it. That experience showed me that the internet is something we can all contribute to; it's been made by people just like you and me.

I decided that I wanted to help build the internet! After studying computer science at university, I worked with technology companies to create apps, games and websites. There I learned that what I loved most was teaching others about how this tech works. I started my own company, and now I get to teach teenagers how to code AI bots, set up servers and help businesses protect themselves from cybercriminals.

So, come with me to discover who and what REALLY makes the internet work. We'll see how millions of computers get connected, where our files and photos live online and how our messages travel across the internet. But we'll also look at the human side of things – who's in charge, how we keep it safe and how it's transformed the way we live. Ready to be an internet explorer? Let's go!

Craig Steele
Technologist, educator and author

INTERNET HISTORY

How and when did the internet begin? It's not like it appeared overnight. In fact, its journey started a lot earlier than you might think. Let's explore how this amazing technological marvel got started.

1960s

The early internet began as a research project funded by the United States government. Scientists and engineers working for the military needed to find a way to connect their computers so they could share information quickly and reliably. This project was called ARPANET (Advanced Research Projects Agency Network) and it was the first step towards creating the internet we know today.

1970s and 1980s

Universities and companies began connecting their computers to the network so that they could share research and knowledge with experts thousands of miles away. Engineers developed new technologies for communicating across the network, including ways to transfer files and send electronic mail, or email!

In the early days of ARPANET, the computers used were massive boxes. Imagine a machine as big as a refrigerator!

The first email

The very first email was sent in 1971 over ARPANET by Ray Tomlinson. He famously used the @ symbol to separate the username from the computer's name, which is why every email address still has that symbol today!

Early orders

Did you know one of the earliest online orders was for a pizza? In 1994, Pizza Hut launched a basic website that let customers choose their toppings online, but they still had to pick it up and pay for it in person!

1990s

By the 1990s people could access the internet from their home computers. The World Wide Web, invented by British scientist Tim Berners-Lee, was launched and people started to visit websites.

Google launched in 1998, making it much easier to find information online – but there were popular search engines before that, including Yahoo!, AltaVista and Ask Jeeves.

2000s

Up until this point, if you wanted to go online your computer had to be connected to your modem or router with a cable. But once Wi-Fi came along, you could roam around with your laptop and still stay connected.

Then by the mid-2000s, social media sites connected people with friends and family, changing how we share our lives online.

2010s and 2020s

Smartphones completely changed how we use the internet. Introduced in the late 2000s, these pocket-sized gadgets really took off in the 2010s. Thanks to iPhones and Android phones, people could suddenly go online from almost anywhere!

Meanwhile, mobile networks raced ahead, jumping from 2G speeds to faster 3G, 4G and eventually 5G.

WHAT IS THE INTERNET?

The basic idea of the internet hasn't changed much over the years – even today, it's still a computer network, just a much bigger one than when it first started. A network is a group of connected computers or devices that communicate with each other.

A network of networks

The internet links networks to one another. That's why it's called the internet – it's an interconnected network of networks. The result is a massive collection of millions of devices across the world sharing data.

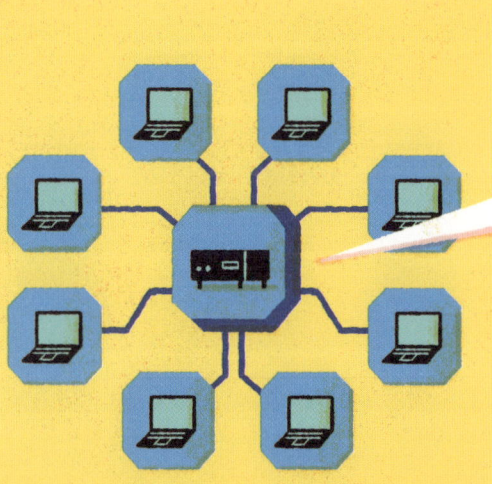

In the middle of a network, a device called a router makes sure the right data is passed between the right computers.

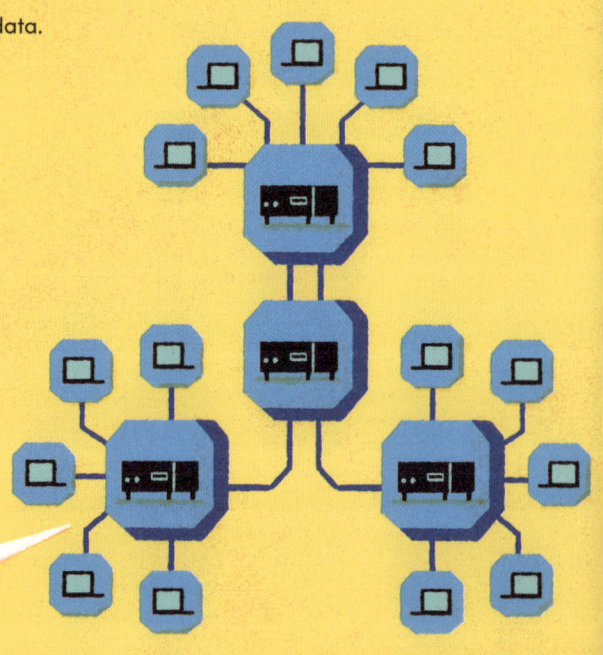

The internet is like this but on a much larger scale, with much bigger routers connecting millions of networks worldwide!

AI AND THE INTERNET

Artificial intelligence (AI) is a type of computer system that is designed to solve problems or make decisions like a human would. It doesn't think or feel like a person – it makes guesses based on patterns found in data. People used to use the internet to do tasks themselves, but now AI can help too.

Changing how we use the internet

Today, people use AI to quickly write messages and summarise long web pages in a flash. Instead of typing questions into search engines, now we find answers using AI chatbots. But remember, AI can get things wrong, so it's smart to double check the answers it comes out with.

Across the internet, AI helps to choose, sort and show you information. Some news sites use AI to show you stories it thinks you'll be interested in, and shops use AI algorithms to promote products that suit you.

How the internet helps train AI

To train a smart AI system, you need lots of data. The biggest AI systems learn from text, pictures, sounds and videos collected from the internet. Think news stories, social media posts, reviews and tutorials. Common Crawl, a library of web pages used to train AI, holds over 250 billion pages. Without the massive amount of information available on the internet, these AI systems wouldn't exist.

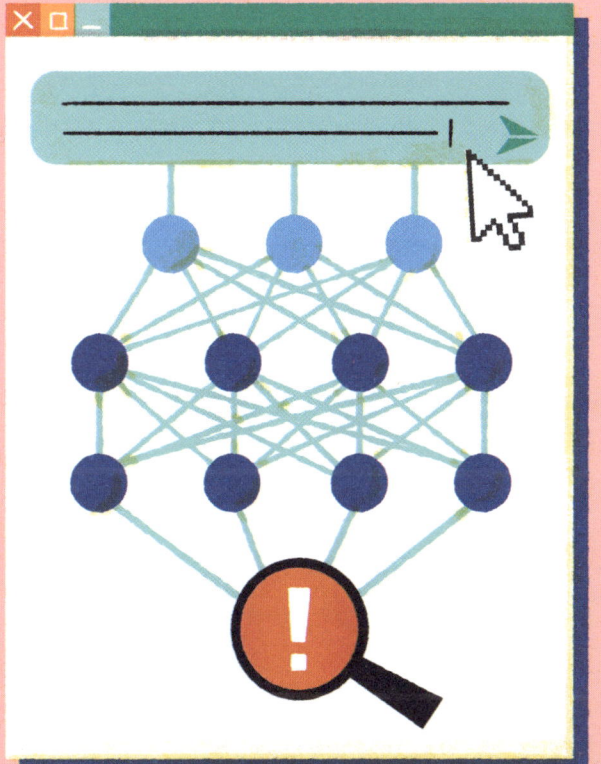

How the internet makes AI possible

Without the internet, we wouldn't be able to use today's AI at all. The biggest systems run on powerful servers in data centres. When your device sends a request over the internet, those servers do the hard work, then the reply comes back in seconds. As more people use AI, a bigger share of internet traffic will be made up of these requests and replies.

THE INFRASTRUCTURE OF THE INTERNET

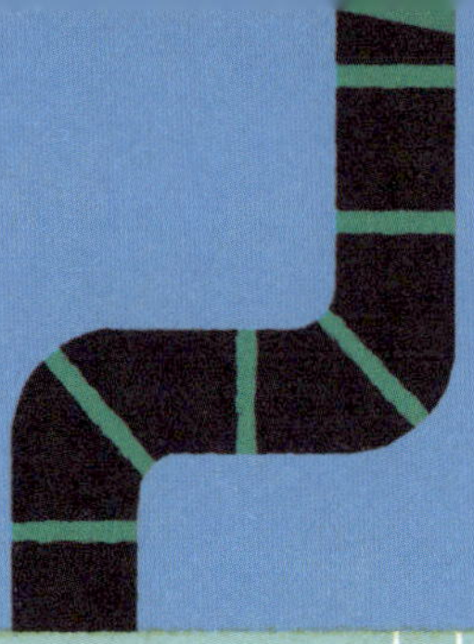

Some parts of the internet you can see easily, like a broadband router at home. But did you know most of the internet's structure is actually hidden? Below the sea there are long lines of cables; above you, thousands of satellites orbit Earth; and dotted around the globe are warehouses full of powerful computers. These work together to form the physical foundation of the internet.

Cables

There are hundreds of thousands of kilometres of internet cables zig-zagging across entire continents, and along the seabed, undersea cables are laid to connect countries and islands. Most of these cables use fibre optic strands, which are super-thin threads of glass that transmit data as pulses of light.

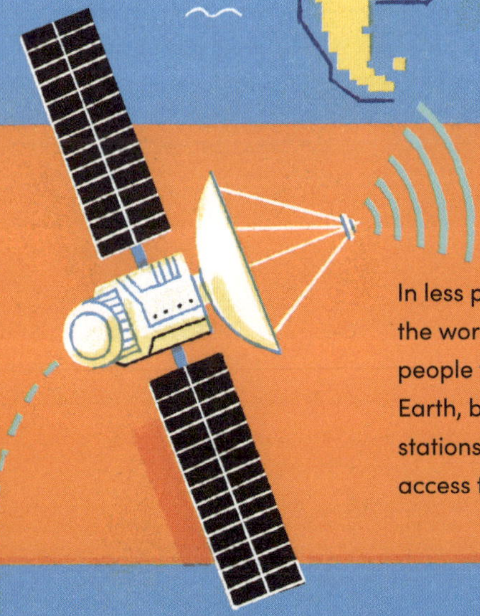

Satellites

In less populated and more rural areas of the world, satellites are used to connect people to the internet. They orbit high above Earth, beaming signals to and from ground stations. These satellites also provide internet access to people travelling in aeroplanes.

5G cell towers

When you use the internet on a phone while out and about, it connects to a nearby cell tower using a high-speed 5G connection. Cell towers are used by mobile network operators, who send your data through their networks before it goes to the internet.

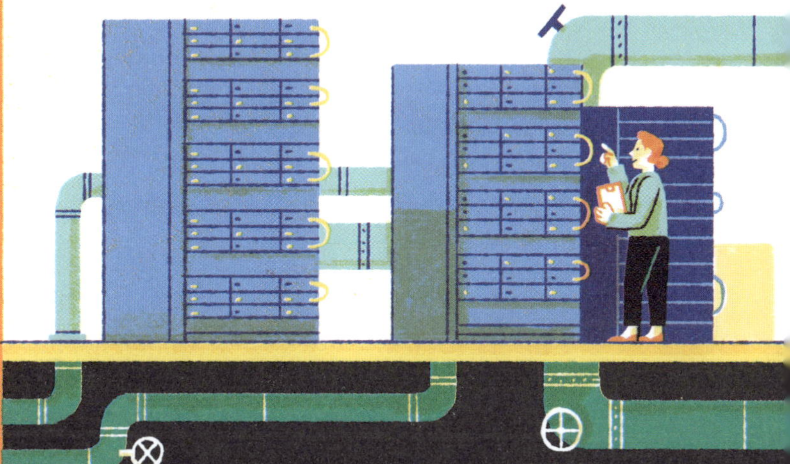

Data centres

A data centre is a giant building filled with powerful computers called servers that store the files, code and databases needed by websites and apps and AI systems. Servers handle millions of requests from across the internet. Data centres have thousands of machines running, which get very hot and need to be cooled constantly. One cooling system can use as much as 4 million litres of water per day – that's the same amount used by a town of 10,000 people!

Home Wi-Fi

All of your devices at home are most likely connected to the internet using a technology called Wi-Fi. Instead of wires or cables, data from your devices is transmitted to a home router using radio waves. The home router gives you access to the internet.

Routers

Routers are like traffic officers – they are computers that help data navigate around busy sections of the internet. When a router receives a packet of data, it forwards it along the right path to its destination. These powerful computers are set up at important junctions across the internet world.

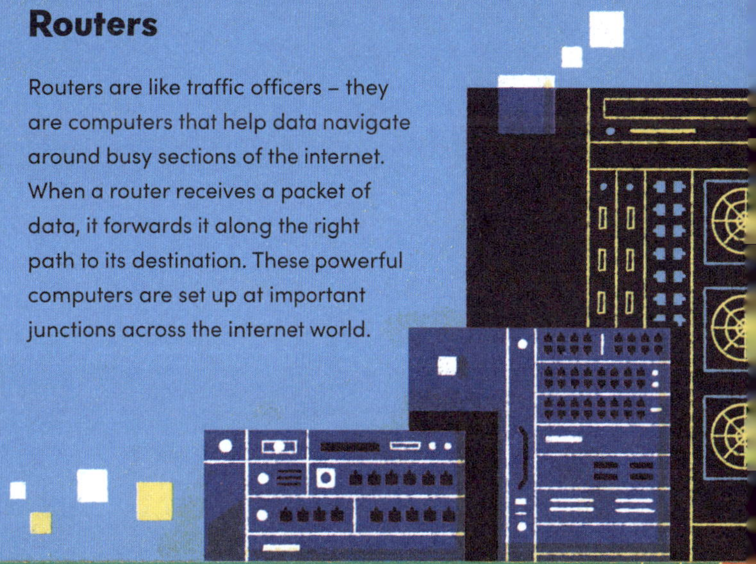

Internet service provider

To connect to the internet at home or work, people pay a company called an internet service provider (ISP) for access. They provide network equipment (like a wireless router) and manage the connection to make sure users have reliable speeds, making getting online a breeze.

Internet exchange points

An internet exchange point (IXP) is a location where different ISPs connect their networks to each other. By sharing traffic, ISPs allow data to take the shortest route across multiple networks. Companies that use the internet sometimes keep copies of popular data at an IXP so that it doesn't have to travel as far to reach people.

HOW DATA IS SENT ACROSS THE INTERNET

Have you ever thought about the journey your emails, chats and YouTube videos take to get to you? Photos, videos and web pages are all just data files. When we transfer data across the internet, each computer involved must follow a set of rules – called the Internet Protocol – to make sure that every file reaches its destination quickly and accurately.

Data on a journey

Rosa wants to download an image of a dragon to use as a cool wallpaper on her phone. Here's how that file is transmitted across the internet, using the Internet Protocol rules:

STEP 1. First, the image is chopped into small packets, which are easier to transfer. A small 1 megabyte image file like this might be broken down into 700 packets.

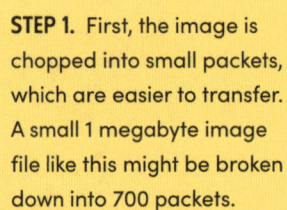

STEP 2. Each packet is made up of two parts. The payload is data from the dragon image file. The header is like a label for the packet, which includes the destination IP address (where the file is going), the origin IP address (where it's being sent from) and other useful information, like how many packets there are in total.

DATA BLAST
WHAT IS AN IP ADDRESS?

Every device connected to the internet is given a unique IP (Internet Protocol) address. This allows the computers, phones, tablets, routers and all other devices connected to the internet to recognise and communicate with each other.

Most of the time, your gadgets get given a different address every time they connect to the internet – called a dynamic IP address – but some computers get an address that never changes – a static IP address.

STEP 4. When all the packets have arrived at their destination IP address they're assembled into the correct order using the information in their headers, creating the photo of the dragon.

Packets travel across the world through the internet in the blink of an eye. For example, a packet can travel from a computer in New York to London in 145 milliseconds.

STEP 3. The packets are sent individually across the internet, where routers forward each packet towards its destination. As they travel, the packets take different paths. Some can even get lost and 'drop' off the network, needing to be retransmitted (sent again).

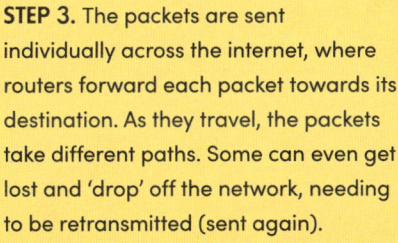

DATA BLAST
WHAT IS BINARY?

Computers only understand electrical signals that are either 'on' or 'off'. We represent those signals using two special numbers: 1 and 0. We call these binary digits, or 'bits' for short. Every file on a computer, laptop or phone is represented using a sequence of bits.

THE PEOPLE WHO KEEP US CONNECTED

It takes teams of people to build, manage and maintain the internet. They work around the clock, making sure everything works every time you go online. These highly skilled people do important, necessary jobs that keep us all connected.

NETWORK ARCHITECTS design the layout of the internet. They plan the best locations to place network equipment and the connections between them, creating the routes for data to travel. They even plan backup routes so if part of the network goes down, data can still get to its destination. Network architects also work directly with equipment, especially when setting up or repairing a network.

The computer systems in a data centre are designed by a **CLOUD ARCHITECT**. They figure out the best ways to store and organise huge amounts of data so it's always ready when you need it. They work alongside **DATA CENTRE TECHNICIANS** to make sure your data – like photos, videos and documents – are stored safely.

DATA BLAST
THE CLOUD

When engineers talk about the Cloud, they mean a massive network of data centres where data and apps are stored online instead of on your computer. It's called the Cloud because, like a cloud floating above, you can't hold or touch it, but you can reach it from anywhere with an internet connection.

TELECOMMUNICATIONS ENGINEERS set up the physical parts of the internet that keep us connected. They work outdoors in all kinds of weather. Some dig trenches to lay kilometres of fibre optic cables, while others climb high towers to install 5G masts for mobile phones. It's these connections that mean the internet can reach even the most remote parts of the country.

An **INTERNET OF THINGS (IOT) ENGINEER** adds internet connectivity to devices we use all the time. For example, your lights at home might be connected to the internet, allowing you to save energy by turning them off remotely when you're not there.

IoT technology is also used on a larger scale. In a 'smart city', traffic lights, street lamps and air quality monitors are connected to the internet to share data and help the city run smoothly.

NETWORK TECHNICIANS work for internet service providers to help their customers get connected to the internet. They might visit your home and help set up a router so your family gets a strong Wi-Fi signal in every room. Or they'll work with businesses to test their internet connection, making sure they get the fastest possible speeds.

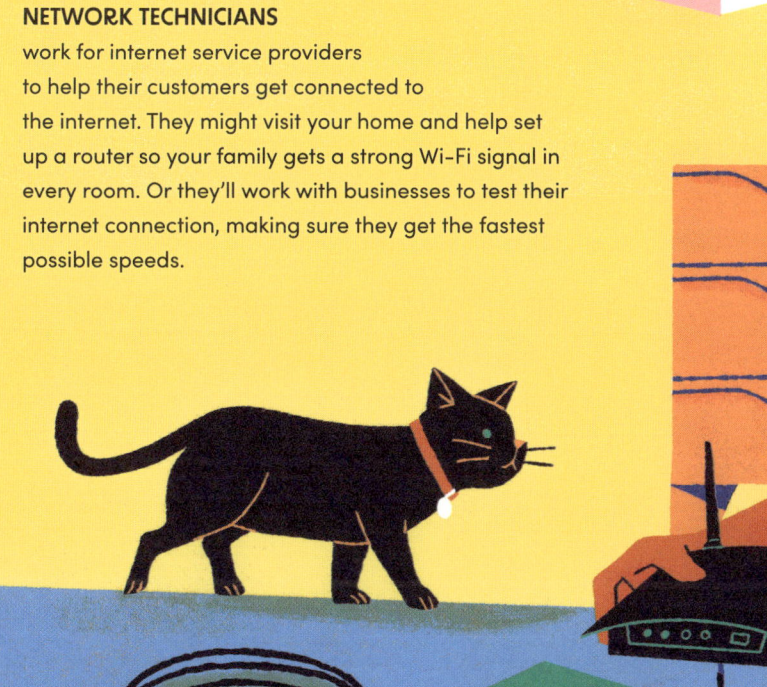

WHO MAKES THE INTERNET?

Millions of people are behind the websites, apps and services we use every day on the internet. They don't all work for tech companies either – these days, every business needs a technology team. From high street shops selling online to restaurants managing reservations and banks handling accounts, skilled tech professionals are behind it all. Let's step inside a tech team's office and meet the people who make it happen.

Check out PhaserFlix, a made-up video streaming company that has a library of science fiction films and TV shows. Customers pay to watch videos on their website, mobile app or on a smart TV. These are the jobs that make it happen:

SOFTWARE ENGINEERS build the app and website. They write the code that underpins the entire service.

FRONT-END ENGINEERS create the code for the parts of a website or app that you see and interact with. For a video streaming app, that's the video player and the features that let you browse or search the library. They write code with front-end programming languages and use tools called frameworks, like React and Angular, to build web apps.

Front-end engineers work on performance optimisation – making sure web pages load quickly even with a slow connection or old computer. One way they do this is by making images download just before you scroll to them, rather than all at once!

BACK-END ENGINEERS develop and maintain the code for the areas of an app or website you don't see. At PhaserFlix, this includes managing databases of videos, making sure the videos load quickly and ensuring that the servers can handle millions of people watching a series at the same time.

Managing servers is a crucial job. If millions of PhaserFlix customers want to stream a new movie, the back-end engineers will bring online, or 'spin up', extra servers to cope with the demand. This is called scaling. When servers deal with lots of requests at once, developers use a technique called load balancing, where they redirect requests to less busy servers.

MACHINE LEARNING ENGINEERS create a tool used by many websites today: the recommendation engine. This is a system that uses AI to predict what customers might want to see using users' data. On PhaserFlix, the recommendation engine suggests the best sci-fi film to watch, while on other sites it might recommend a new song to add to your playlist. This is a really important system for lots of online businesses, because the better the recommendation engine is at making suggestions, the more likely someone is to keep using a website.

All by design

Did you know that every image, icon and layout on a website or app is carefully chosen? The User Experience (UX) team plan and design the parts of web apps and websites we interact with.

USER EXPERIENCE DESIGNERS plan how a website looks, plus how it feels to use too! Is it fun and easy to use, or is there an area people get stuck on? These designers tackle these questions as they create.

WEB DESIGNERS create the look of a website or app. They decide the layout, carefully choosing colours, fonts and images to make everything come together visually. They often use software like Photoshop, Figma and XD to create and test out different layout ideas.

I designed this floating video player. You can move, resize or close it whenever you want. I made sure it didn't get in the way of the user's experience!

USER EXPERIENCE RESEARCHERS find ways to make websites easier to use. By watching how users navigate their site, they identify problems and pass them along to the design team, who make improvements. A UX researcher might create two versions of a webpage that asks users to make a new account. They'll measure how long it takes people to fill out each form to see which version was quicker and easier to complete. This technique is called A/B testing.

ACCESSIBILITY SPECIALISTS make sure websites and apps can be used by everyone, including people with disabilities. They create features which remove barriers that hinder some users' experiences, for example, closed captions for people who are deaf or hard of hearing and audio descriptions for people with low vision.

How web apps are designed

The design process for a website or app is a loop – once it starts, the UX team goes through the steps again and again.

The UX team talks to users to find out what they like and dislike. They also try out apps made by other companies to see what makes them easy to use.

The UX team decides what features the app should have based on what users want and need. This makes sure the app will be useful and enjoyable.

Once the app is out, researchers find out what people think of it. Can they work it? What problems are they having? They listen to what users are saying and keep working on the app to make it even better.

1. RESEARCH
2. DEFINE
3. DESIGN
4. TEST
5. IMPLEMENT
6. LAUNCH
7. EVALUATE

Designers sketch how the app might look on different devices, like a laptop, tablet or phone. They plan where the most important features go and which colours and icons to use.

Developers release the app so users can use it!

Developers build the next version of the app.

Researchers ask a small group of users to use a prototype version of the app and give feedback. If anything confuses them, they make a note to fix it!

19

PROGRAMMING LANGUAGES

If you want to understand how the web works, you need to explore the computer code behind each page. You'll see that web developers use a combination of programming languages to create amazing websites. That's right – different languages do specific jobs to help a website work smoothly.

Speaking the right language

Coding languages are divided into two types:

FRONT-END LANGUAGES are used to write the code that creates the parts of websites you see and interact with in your web browser. This includes the layout, design, buttons and menus.

BACK-END LANGUAGES are used to write the code that runs behind the scenes on the server. They handle important tasks like data storage, user logins and processing orders.

HTML and CSS

Every web page uses two important front-end languages: HTML (HyperText Markup Language) and CSS (Cascading Style Sheets). They are known as markup languages as they set out (mark up) instructions for how a web page should look.

HTML is like the skeleton of a webpage – it's used to make the structure of the page and the things that go on it, including headings, images, paragraphs of text, and buttons.

CSS lists the instructions for how those different parts of the page should look, such as what fonts and colours should be used and where they should be placed on the page.

```html
HTML
<!DOCTYPE html>
<html lang="en">
<head>
    <link rel="stylesheet" href="styles.css">
    <title>My First Web Page</title>
</head>
<body>
    <h1>Welcome to My Web Page</h1>
    <p>This is a paragraph of text that gives some information.</p>
    <button>Click Me!</button>
</body>
</html>
```

This HTML markup code is for a heading, a paragraph and a button.

```css
CSS
body {
    background-color: lightblue;
    font-family: Arial, sans-serif;
}
h1 {
    color: darkblue;
    text-align: center;
}
p {
    color: darkgray;
    font-size: 16px;
}
button {
    background-color: darkblue;
    color: white;
    border: none;
    padding: 10px 20px;
    cursor: pointer;
}
```

This CSS code sets the colours, fonts and button appearance. When the HTML and CSS are linked together it creates a web page.

Making websites interactive

JavaScript is the most popular front-end programming language. It brings web pages to life by making them interactive (reacting to users' actions). It can check if a form is filled out correctly, create menus that open and close, and upload photos or videos to posts. Anytime you interact with a web page – whether you swipe, press a button or type something in – that's JavaScript at work!

Connecting to databases

Databases on servers store information that websites need, like users' account details and lists of products. Web developers use a back-end language called SQL (Structured Query Language) to request information from the database or to add, remove or update entries.

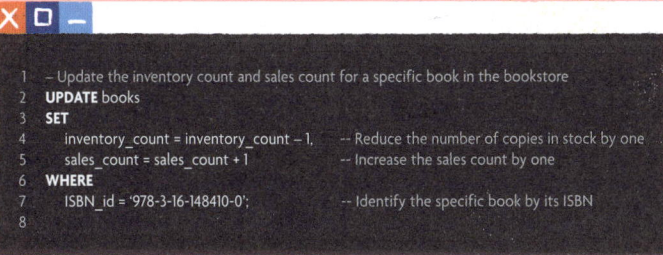

When a customer orders a book, an SQL command is sent to the database to update the entry for that item, reducing the number of stock by one.

Coding dynamic websites

PHP is another back-end programming language web developers love using because it can automatically create web pages for them. Imagine an online bookshop with thousands of books to sell. Instead of making a separate webpage for each book, developers create a template page with spaces for the title, price and description. When a user clicks on a book, the PHP code runs alongside SQL commands to grab the correct details from the database, fill in the template and send the finished page back to the user.

ON ASSIGNMENT
CHECK OUT SOME FRONT-END CODE

Did you know you can peek behind any website to see its HTML and CSS code? Here's how to do it:

1. Open a website that you trust in your browser. Always browse safely and with an adult's permission.
2. Right-click on the page and select 'Inspect' or 'View Page Source' from the menu.
3. A panel will open, showing you the HTML and CSS code used to build that page!
4. Explore the code to see how different elements are styled and structured.

OPEN SOURCE TECHNOLOGY

Behind every app and website is **source code**. This is the collection of computer code that controls the app or site. **Closed source** means the code is private and details about how it works are hidden. This can be to prevent other people from copying it or trying to break it. Open source means the code has been shared for anyone to look at, experiment with or turn into something new.

Sharing is caring

What's so special about open source? Well, plainly, sharing code for free can speed up new tech breakthroughs. Anyone and everyone – from solo coders to giant companies – can jump in and help at any time to make the internet even better. Being able to freely remix and reuse other people's code and discover new ways to make it work is the reason internet technology improves so rapidly.

The open source community

Some of the most important tools we use on the internet are open source projects...

Tens of millions of web servers use an open source software called Apache to host and manage websites.

The Firefox web browser is used by millions for its speed and privacy features.

Nearly half of all websites in the world are built using an open source app called WordPress.

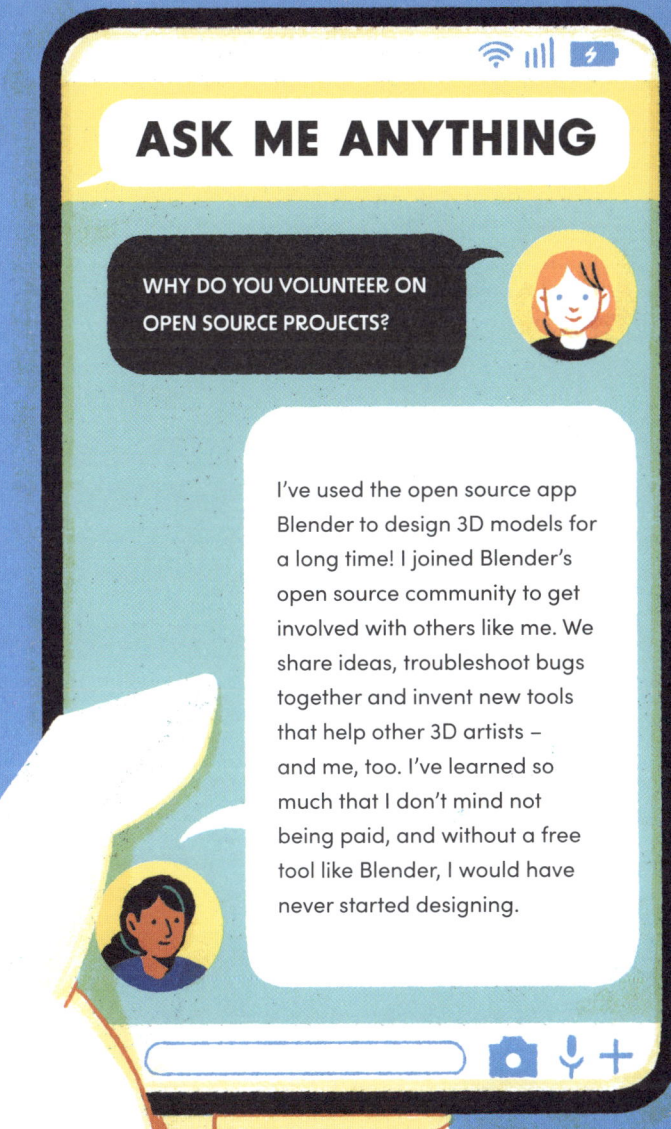

ASK ME ANYTHING

WHY DO YOU VOLUNTEER ON OPEN SOURCE PROJECTS?

I've used the open source app Blender to design 3D models for a long time! I joined Blender's open source community to get involved with others like me. We share ideas, troubleshoot bugs together and invent new tools that help other 3D artists – and me, too. I've learned so much that I don't mind not being paid, and without a free tool like Blender, I would have never started designing.

... and many people all over the world volunteer their time and skills to work on them. These people are called open source contributors. Some are software engineers who use open source code to build their own apps. They study how the code works, add their own features, then share the updated code so everyone can benefit from it.

But not every open source contributor is a coding genius. Some focus on writing documentation – instructions for how people should use the code. Others speak with people and businesses who use apps made with the open source code to gather ideas on how to improve it. It's a real team effort!

The problem with open source

Working on an open source project takes a lot of time and effort. While it can feel rewarding to make a better internet for everyone, some people benefit more than others. Big tech companies like Google, Amazon and Meta can include open source code as part of the products they sell without having to pay the people who work on it. In turn, they end up making money off passionate people working for free.

Open source projects also face a risk of abandonment. Volunteers can stop contributing at any point, either because they lose interest in the project or become too busy in other parts of their lives. Is it smart for tech companies to rely so heavily on volunteers to maintain some of the internet's most critical apps? To keep these important projects going, we may need to find better ways to support open source contributors, including encouraging companies to pay them for their work.

23

HOW THE INTERNET CHANGED SHOPPING

E-commerce is the name for buying and selling things online. Nowadays, regular shoppers love shopping from home – whether buying from massive stores or small businesses. E-commerce companies use internet technology to manage online stores, process payments and target adverts to the right customers.

E-commerce platforms

Starting a shop used to mean renting a space, filling it with products and selling them to people who walked in. But now a shop can be set up completely online. People use e-commerce platforms like Shopify, Magento and WooCommerce to help build the website for their online stores, so they can show off their products and take payments.

Online marketplaces

Online marketplaces let regular people list items, and buyers can bid for them or buy them. Etsy lets people sell handmade crafts, while eBay is great for selling things you no longer use. It's a great way to keep things out of landfills and pass them on to someone who will appreciate them.

Targeted advertising

Ever felt like an advert is following you around the internet? E-commerce companies use technology called targeted advertising to show you items you've looked at before.

Cookies are small files that track what pages you visit and what products you view. This data gets shared with advertising companies, who use this information to show you ads they think you'll like. If that feels creepy, you can block these trackers by blocking cookies.

How online payments work

When someone buys something online, how does that money get from their bank account to the seller? Here's a simple explanation:

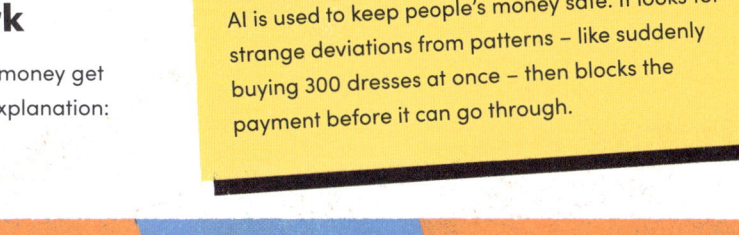

DATA BLAST
AI FRAUD DETECTION
AI is used to keep people's money safe. It looks for strange deviations from patterns – like suddenly buying 300 dresses at once – then blocks the payment before it can go through.

Theo buys a pair of £20 sunglasses from Kirstie's shop. He provides his bank details and VISA card information. VISA is a company that helps move money between banks.

Stripe, the payment processor, asks VISA to check if Theo has enough money in his account.

VISA contacts Theo's bank to confirm he can pay.

Theo's bank approves the transaction, and £20 is reserved from his account.

Kirstie's shop shows Theo an order confirmation and she sends him the sunglasses.

Stripe sends the £20 to Kirstie's account.

VISA tells Stripe the payment was successful and transfers the £20.

Theo's bank sends £20 to VISA.

Changes for better or worse

In many ways, the internet has made shopping a better experience. But there are downsides too.

- Instead of being limited to what's in our local shops, we can order anything from groceries to a brand-new car.

- Other customers' reviews help us figure out if a product is right for us – or one to avoid.

- Shops use AI recommendation engines to suggest new things to buy based on what we've looked at or bought before.

- Online shopping makes it super easy to buy stuff we don't actually need – everything's cheaper and faster to get. That's called overconsumption.

- Products come from all over the world, and that uses more fuel, which isn't great for the environment. They're also wrapped in extra packaging to protect them, but that means more waste too.

- Dodgy online sellers offer fake products, including food, electronics and makeup. These counterfeit items might look real but can be harmful or dangerous.

HOW THE INTERNET CHANGED THE WAY WE LEARN

What if your classmate could join your lesson from Antarctica? Or that you could have a cooking lesson from a teacher in Italy? Well, today, these things are entirely possible thanks to the internet!

A classroom without walls

Internet technology can create an experience that's a lot like being in a classroom, even if you're not physically there.

Lessons can be recorded or taught live through apps like Zoom or Microsoft Teams, which allow for big video calls.

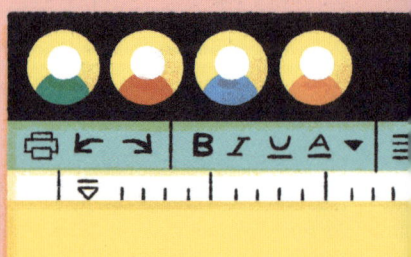

Web apps like Microsoft Office 365 or Google Docs let everyone work on the same document at the same time.

In our class, an AI app records our group chats and turns them into notes. It's great for going back over lessons later.

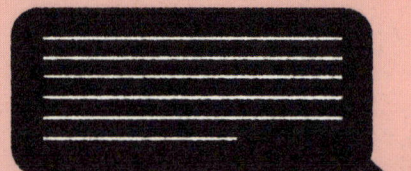

Online courses for everyone

Online school isn't just for kids. Famous universities like Cambridge and Harvard have online courses, and websites like Khan Academy and Coursera let people learn all kinds of subjects, from philosophy to graphic design. Ever heard of MOOCs? There's no limit to how many people can join a Massive Open Online Course – they're huge!

Digital badges

There was a time when people thought online qualifications weren't real, but some A-grade internet tech has changed that! Digital badges prove that you've completed a course or earned a qualification. You can share them on your social media and attach them to job applications.

Each badge has a unique, unchangeable link called a credential URL. The link connects to a database that shows who issued the badge, when it was earned and what skills or qualifications it represents. Some even use blockchain technology, which makes it nearly impossible to fake.

Visual learning

If you're reading this book, you know that school isn't the only way to learn. Online, creators on YouTube and TikTok make videos that teach you subjects you might not learn at school. Some videos are made by teachers, but many are created by passionate people who love sharing their interests. If you're stuck on your homework, these edu-taining videos might be for you!

Information at your fingertips

We gather and share information on the internet at lightning-fast speeds. Check out Project Gutenberg – an online library with over 70,000 free ebooks anyone can download. Amazingly, it started before the internet even existed.

And I bet you have used Wikipedia, a free online encyclopaedia that people from all over the world create and update together. Unlike books that need new editions to add or fix information, Wikipedia can be updated instantly. However, because anyone can edit a page, sometimes it has mistakes or false information.

Luckily, people watch out for these problems. A Wikipedia rollbacker quickly undoes changes made by other users to stop inappropriate edits to articles. New page patrollers make sure new entries aren't misleading or wrong.

HOW THE INTERNET CHANGED VIDEO GAMES

Gaming has been popular for decades, but the internet has taken it to a whole new level. In the late 90s, games like *Quake* and *Age of Empires* let players around the world challenge each other online, just like *Minecraft* and *Roblox* today! But without fast internet connections and powerful servers, these games wouldn't be possible.

How do online game servers work?

When you play online, a game server keeps track of everything happening in the game. It's constantly sending and receiving information from players' computers or consoles all over the world, like characters' locations, levels or items. This combined data is called the game state. The server shares it with all players, keeping everyone's game synchronised.

Cloud gaming

Cloud gaming lets gamers play their games on powerful machines owned by tech companies. Games run remotely on the high-performance hardware and are streamed back to players. If you've got a fast connection, this saves you from needing an expensive gaming setup at home.

DATA BLAST
LAG

Ever had your game stutter or your character randomly jump when playing online? That's called lag – it's a delay in data being sent between the game server and your device.

Patch that!

On physical game cartridges, when game developers made a mistake, every single copy would have that problem. There was no easy fix! Now, thanks to the internet, when a bug is found, people called game maintainers create a patch to fix it.

A patch targets specific lines of code or swaps out files to correct the problem. The patch file is uploaded to the game server then downloaded by your game. Patches are rolled out in waves to avoid overwhelming servers, sometimes taking up to a day to reach all players.

Stopping piracy

Piracy is when people make a copy of or play a game they don't have permission to – something the internet has made easier, as uploading a file and sharing it takes seconds. To combat this, Digital Rights Management (DRM) technology was invented. When you open a game with DRM, it checks if you have a licence to play it. When the game server confirms you do, it sends a signal back that unlocks the game and lets you play.

DATA BLAST
CATCHING CHEATERS

In an online game, you can't look over someone's shoulder to spot cheating, so game companies fight back with anti-cheat software that uses AI to watch players' moves. If it sees something impossible – like clicking improbably fast – it alerts the game moderators, who can warn or ban players who break the rules.

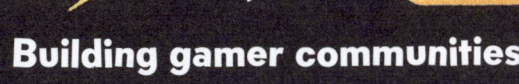

Building gamer communities

Discord is an online messaging platform built by two friends who loved to game together but couldn't find an easy way to chat when playing. Discord servers let people all over the world chat using text, voice or video. Server owners can also use AI bots to help them manage the server, programming them to do tasks like welcome new members, play music or keep track of player stats.

HOW THE INTERNET CHANGED THE MUSIC INDUSTRY

It wasn't long ago that when you wanted to listen to music, you either had to turn on the radio or buy an album on a cassette tape, vinyl record or CD. But the internet has changed the way we enjoy music, and how we make it too! Music can be transferred through the internet in a flash, and this has meant big changes for the music industry.

A digital music revolution

Introducing: Napster, a file-sharing service. In the late 1990s, people used Napster to download music for free from each other's computers. Eventually, Napster was shut down because it's illegal for people to share files without the copyright owner's permission, but it showed there was a huge demand for digital downloads of music.

Downloading and streaming

Apple's iTunes Store opened in 2003 and let fans buy music downloads online. Music fans could pay for any individual track, rather than buying a full album. Then, at the close of the decade, Spotify changed people's music buying habits once again. People could stream whatever songs they wanted from a massive library for a monthly fee.

Helping musicians reach new audiences

In the past, musicians needed a record label to have any hope of reaching a wide audience. But web-based platforms like SoundCloud, YouTube and Bandcamp let people upload their songs without a record deal. Social media, like TikTok, helps smaller artists connect with fans and promote their music for free!

But the shift to streaming has meant challenges for musicians too. The most popular streaming apps only pay between $3 to $5 for every 1,000 plays of a track. Despite reaching bigger audiences than ever before, often artists aren't making much money.

How music apps stream songs

Music streaming apps make it look easy! You pick a track and you can listen to it instantly in high quality. But there's some incredible tech behind the music.

DATA COMPRESSION
Smaller files take less time to travel across the internet, so streaming apps use a technique called compression to shrink the size of each song. They remove parts of the sound that our ears can't hear, so the file size is reduced but to our ears it doesn't sound any different.

ADAPTIVE BIT RATE
Streaming apps change the bit rate of the audio stream based on your internet speed. If your connection slows down, the app lowers the bit rate to prevent buffering, so your music keeps playing smoothly.

PRELOADING
Often, parts of popular songs are downloaded before you even hit play. This is why songs start playing so quickly — they're already stored on your device!

AUDIO STREAMS
Each track is stored as a file on servers all around the world. When you play a song, the app grabs chunks of the file from the closest server. Each chunk is typically 512 kilobytes in size, about 25 seconds of audio. At your device, they're put back together to create a seamless audio stream.

DATA BLAST
BIT RATE
Bit rate is the amount of data processed per second in a music file. A higher bit rate means better quality audio.

USER-GENERATED CONTENT

It used to be the norm to get all our information and entertainment from big media companies. They were the ones with the tools needed to create books, newspapers, music and movies, and had the know-how to share it with huge audiences. But now, anyone with a phone or computer can create something and share it with the world! We call this user-generated content.

DATA BLAST
AI-GENERATED CONTENT

Not all online content is made by people! AI apps generate images, videos and more. But who should get the credit for what a machine makes? And if AI can do creative work, what does that mean for humans? These big questions are shaping the future of the internet.

We make the web

Many social media sites don't actually make their own content – they need us to upload ours. Social media sites would be totally empty without our posts. Even meme pages wouldn't exist without people creating and sharing funny content. If these sites make money from things we share, do you think they should pay us, or is getting to use the site for free enough?

Everyone can be a creator

In the early days, if you wanted to share something online, you had to know how to build a web page. Then new websites like GeoCities and Piczo made it easy for anyone to create web pages of their own. Social media sites simplified uploading photos, music and videos, and suddenly everyone had the tools to create and share something on the web.

DATA BLAST
WEB 2.0

When user-generated content started to take off, this was such a big change in the way people used the internet that people began calling it 'Web 2.0'.

32

Helping people be heard

User-generated content gives a voice to people who might not usually be heard. Traditional media is hard to break into, but user-generated content doesn't have the same barriers. A poet could post a video of themselves performing their latest work, or a teenager might vlog about life in their small town. A refugee can even tell their story, giving us a glimpse into worlds we don't otherwise see.

Breaking the news

User-generated content also has a role to play in our news cycle: social media sites buzz with the latest updates as soon as it happens. When there's a big event, users post photos and updates straight to social media for others to read and share. Sometimes they even break stories too! Being able to post instantly means important stories can reach people around the world long before traditional news outlets.

Can you rely on it?

Anyone can post anything online, which means there's a wide range in the quality and accuracy of what you'll see. Some user-generated content is well made and researched, but other content might be full of misinformation or be completely fake. Before you take something as fact, check the sources (where the information came from), see if it's backed up by evidence and consider whether the creator might have a bias or agenda for posting it.

Who made this?!

Do you find it annoying when people copy you? I bet you do, and copying is a problem online too. Content creators need to respect copyright laws, which say you can't use someone else's work without permission.

Sometimes well-known companies get caught red-handed stealing ideas too. Some companies have found designs online for T-shirts or jewellery and copied them without asking. They then sell these items, making money off someone else's hard work. How would you feel if someone else became rich or famous from your idea?

HOW CREATORS MAKE MONEY

We've seen how businesses use the internet to make money, but what about creators? Bloggers, podcasters, streamers and vloggers are building huge audiences online. But how do they turn a fun hobby into something that actually pays the bills? It turns out there are many ways for creators to profit from their passion!

Time for an ad break

Often, before YouTube videos and during podcast breaks, there will be an advertisement to watch or listen to. Online tools like Google's AdSense match adverts with creators' audiences. For instance, an ad for a new phone might be interesting to viewers of a YouTuber that reviews tech. Creators get paid to let these adverts run before or during their content, but they don't always get to choose which ones show up.

Collaborations and sponsorships

Think about the people you follow online – you probably trust their opinions. So if they recommend something, you'd probably check it out, right? For example, if a company spots a popular gaming streamer, they might partner with them to promote their products. They know that if the gamer is seen using their headset, their followers are more likely to want one too. The company might pay the gamer to show the product in action. This is called a sponsored post.

Being honest about ads

If a creator is being paid to promote a product, they should be upfront about it. In some countries it's the law. It helps prevent people from being misled by hidden adverts. Creators should clearly label any content that they're being paid to make, so you can decide if it's something you're truly interested in.

#Ad #Sponsor

DATA BLAST
AFFILIATE LINKS

Creators use special links to direct their audiences to products. When followers click on them and make a purchase, the creator earns a small percentage of the sale.

34

Nano-influencers

You don't need millions of followers to make money on the internet. Nano-influencers are creators with fewer than 10,000 followers. Their content is aimed at a small group of people who really care about a certain niche. They often partner with really specific companies who make products aimed at a small number of people.

Selling directly to fans

Creators don't always partner with other companies to make money – they can sell merchandise like hoodies, mugs and stickers, or even custom art pieces or music. Superfans are willing to pay a lot to have something created just for them. Some creators offer subscriptions, where fans pay monthly for behind-the-scenes videos or early access to new content.

ON ASSIGNMENT
IT'S YOUR TURN TO BE THE INFLUENCER

If you were a creator, what would you want to share with the world? Follow the steps below and plan out what your online career might look like.

1. PICK YOUR MESSAGE
What do you love doing or talking about? Maybe you'd teach people how to bake, review your favourite games or raise awareness about protecting the planet.

2. CHOOSE YOUR PLATFORM
How would you share your message? Would you write a blog, film videos or create a podcast? Think about what would work best with your personality – are you in front of the camera or behind it? Are you a writer or a talker?

3. PLAN YOUR FIRST POST
Write down your ideas and think about what will make your message stand out and get people to pay attention! A catchy heading or title, or a special video effect could do the trick.

WHO CONTROLS THE INTERNET?

No one person or company owns or controls the internet, or can switch it off completely. This is called decentralisation. It was built this way, so everyone could share information freely. But there are power struggles on the internet. Companies are fighting to influence us and control what we do online.

The giants of the internet

Although the internet is still decentralised, the way we use it has changed. Most of what we do online is based around a handful of popular websites and apps which are owned by just a few technology companies.

Meta
Facebook
Instagram
Threads
WhatsApp
Messenger

Alphabet
Google
Gmail
YouTube
Android

Amazon
Twitch
Amazon.com
Amazon Web Services (AWS)

Meta controls many of the most popular social networking sites and messenger apps. That means they hold millions of people's personal information.

Practically everyone uses Google search, so being in charge of how this works gives Alphabet lots of power.

Almost one-third of the internet's behind-the-scenes systems are powered by AWS, so Amazon could have influence and power over other companies.

DATA BLAST
WALLED GARDENS

Some social media apps are like walled gardens because they control what you can see and do. You're free to play, but only inside that space! YouTube is a walled garden because creators can't easily move their videos or subscribers to another platform.

Who's really in charge?

On social media, it might feel like you're in charge – liking and following posts and accounts that make you smile and skipping the ones that don't. But a lot of what you see online is picked for you by an algorithm.

Tech companies want you to spend as much time on their app as possible, so they use AI to guess what kind of posts will keep you watching. This type of AI is designed to show you things you'll enjoy or agree with, which can trap you in a filter bubble where you only see posts that match your own interests and opinions. While that can feel good, it means you might miss out on different perspectives or important news.

What can we do about it?

Some people think it's not fair that we've given so much power to just a handful of technology companies. Here are some ways we can give more control back to users.

Require messaging apps to let us chat with friends across different platforms.

This is called cross-platform compatibility.

Make companies make our data more portable.

This is so we can easily move our photos, friends and other information between services.

Teach people about self-hosting.

This is where users run their own services. For example, a school could manage its own video-sharing platform instead of relying on YouTube.

Create communities where users can vote on big updates or changes.

In an online game, players could vote to decide which features to improve or remove. This shares decision-making power with users.

HOW FAIR IS THE INTERNET?

When we say something is neutral, that means it doesn't pick a side. It's fair and treats everyone the same. Net neutrality is all about letting all people have the freedom to access internet data equally, rather than letting tech companies and internet service providers have control over who can access it, how and when.

Being fair to everyone

Supporters of net neutrality think that ISPs should treat all legal internet activity the same. They shouldn't give special treatment to certain websites, block people from areas of the internet or allow people faster and better access because they are willing to pay more.

But critics think the net neutrality rules are too strict. People use the internet for different reasons – you might be watching YouTube while somewhere else, the internet is being used to share news of a natural disaster. Are these things as important as each other, or do some things need special attention?

Rules for a fairer internet

To make things more complicated when it comes to governing the internet, there isn't one rule that applies around the world. Each country has its own laws that say how ISPs should handle net neutrality. Here are some of the most common rules:

RULE 1: NO THROTTLING

If you love streaming, you know a fast internet connection is important. But this causes a lot of data traffic. Because of this, an ISP might want to slow down your internet speed – this is called throttling. You then might want to pay more for your speeds to not be limited. Net neutrality rules say all traffic should be treated equally.

RULE 2: NO BLOCKING

Net neutrality says you should have the freedom to visit any website or online service without your ISP stopping you. Of course, sometimes an ISP needs to block a website, for example, if it's illegal, but they can't block you from somewhere they'd rather you didn't visit, like a rival company's website.

RULE 3: NO TRICKY BUSINESS DEALS

Imagine someone is buying a new pair of trainers, when suddenly, as they click the buy button, they're taken to a different shop. Why? Because that shop has a deal with their ISP and gives them money for every sale. Net neutrality rules say you should be able to choose where you shop without your ISP trying to make money from it.

What do you think?

There's an ongoing debate around net neutrality. Have a look at different people's opinions and see where you stand.

Net neutrality is crucial to my small business. It means my website has the same chance of reaching customers as bigger businesses.

Mike
ONLINE PET FOOD SHOP OWNER

I have mixed feelings about net neutrality. Streaming takes up a lot of bandwidth. It's responsible for more than half of the internet's traffic worldwide, so some customers end up paying more to support heavy streamers. It feels a little unfair.

Lisa
INTERNET SERVICE PROVIDER EMPLOYEE

Net neutrality helps me spread the message about climate change. ISPs can't make it harder for activists to share important news by slowing their websites or making them pay extra.

Sophie
CLIMATE ADVOCATE

Net neutrality is a must for gamers. No one wants to lose a game just because their connection is being slowed down on purpose!

Alex
A PROFESSIONAL ESPORTS GAMER

If we paid a little more based on what we actually do online, ISPs could use that extra cash to invest in research and improving the infrastructure. That could mean faster speeds and more reliable internet for everyone.

Ajay
TELECOMS NETWORK ENGINEER

CYBERCRIME ON THE INTERNET

How safe is the internet? Most of our experiences using it are positive, but there is a darker – sometimes dangerous – side to being online. As more people use the internet for shopping and banking, criminals find more chances to steal money and personal information. But there are ways we can protect ourselves and stay safe online.

Malware most wanted

One way to protect ourselves from cybercrime is to understand what it looks like. Malware, short for 'malicious software', is used to attack computer systems, destroy data or steal personal information. It can come in a few forms:

VIRUS

A virus spreads by infecting other files or sending copies of itself through emails and chats between contacts. Viruses can be used to steal sensitive information or delete important files.

TROJAN HORSE

Sometimes malware hides inside an innocent-looking app or game. When you try to use it, the virus is activated. It's named after the famous Greek myth where soldiers snuck into Troy inside a wooden horse.

RANSOMWARE

Ransomware locks you out of a computer system and blocks you from accessing your files. Criminals then demand money (a ransom) to let you back in.

Hacking the human

It's much easier to trick a human than it is to break into a computer, so sometimes if a criminal wants certain information, they'll try to trick a person into making their computer less secure. This is called phishing, and here's how it might happen:

Imagine a cybercriminal wanted access to an email account, they might set a trap that allows them to obtain the password. This is done by creating convincing emails pretending to be from someone's family or friends, or by posing as a trustworthy company and creating a realistic-looking website. Criminals use trust to reel you in and gain your information, so keep an eye out for suspicious messages and friend requests or offers that are too good to be true.

The dark web

The internet is also used by criminals who want to buy and sell illegal goods or carry out harmful acts. Weapons and dangerous materials are traded in underground markets on a part of the internet called the dark web. These illegal websites are hidden from search engines, and can only be visited using special software. The traders use tools to try and make themselves untraceable, to try and avoid being caught.

Who protects us from cybercrime?

Lucky for us, there are thousands of people whose job is to protect us from cybercriminals.

ETHICAL HACKERS

hack into computer systems, but they're not criminals! Companies ask them to find weak spots in their online systems. The hackers report their findings and security teams fix the problems to prevent cybercrime.

DIGITAL FORENSICS SPECIALISTS

work with the police to gather evidence and help solve cybercrimes. Rather than dusting for fingerprints, they pull information from computers' storage or analyse server logs for criminal activity.

CYBER THREAT RESEARCHERS

study how criminals attack computer systems and try to spot common patterns or weaknesses. This research helps security experts invent new techniques to tackle cybercrime.

ON ASSIGNMENT
PROTECT YOURSELF FROM CYBERCRIME

You can also protect yourself and your family from cybercriminals. Complete this checklist to strengthen your digital security, then help your family to follow the steps too. Supporting others to stay safe online makes you a good digital citizen.

1. USE STRONG PASSWORDS FOR ALL YOUR ACCOUNTS

Make them long and use random words so they are hard to guess.

2. CHECK YOU HAVE ANTIVIRUS SOFTWARE INSTALLED ON YOUR COMPUTERS

Most computers have antivirus software built in – you just need to make sure it's activated.

3. MAKE SURE YOUR APPS ARE UP TO DATE

Updating your apps to the latest version helps patch any security problems.

41

ENCRYPTION

Tech companies have another technique to keep our personal information safe and secure on the internet. It's called encryption, and it stops cybercriminals (or anyone else for that matter!) from being able to see things like your private chats with friends, your family photos or sensitive information like your medical records or banking details. It's so clever – it makes this information unreadable!

How encryption works

Encryption software scrambles files so that no one else can view or change them. It works by using a mathematical function that changes the file's data into a mixed-up form. Then the data is locked by something called an encryption key. This key can be created with a password, passcode or biometric data like a fingerprint or face scan. Encryption is powerful because once a file is encrypted, it's basically impossible to access without the key.

Where encryption is used

Encryption is used all over the internet to keep many kinds of information safe.

PRIVATE CONVERSATIONS
Encryption is used on messaging and video calling platforms to create a secure communication channel, stopping people from snooping on you when you're messaging your mates or video calling your grandparents

PROTECTING YOUR PERSONAL FILES
When you store files online in places like iCloud, Google Drive and other storage servers, encryption is used to protect your files from unauthorised people trying to access them.

KEEPING YOUR WEB BROWSING SAFE
Web browsers encrypt the data that is passed between your computer and the website you're on. When you log into a website or buy something online, encryption protects your password and payment information while it's being sent. When you see 'https' in the address bar of your web browser, encryption is creating a secure connection.

WIRELESS NETWORKS
Do you use a password to connect to your Wi-Fi at home? If so, your Wi-Fi network uses encryption too. It protects the data being sent and received from all the devices connected to it.

Sending messages securely

You might wonder, if your messages get scrambled, how can someone on the receiving end read them? Lots of messenger apps use a technique called end-to-end encryption, meaning messages are encrypted and decrypted on each side of the conversation.

STEP 1. The messenger app creates two encryption keys – a public key and a private key. Anything that is encrypted using your public key can only be decrypted using your private key. Your private key is never shared with anyone.

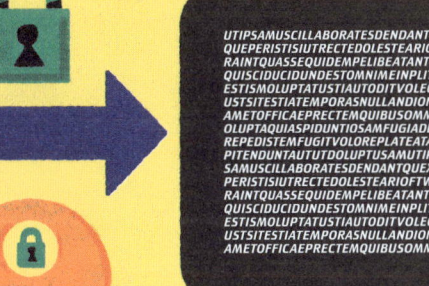
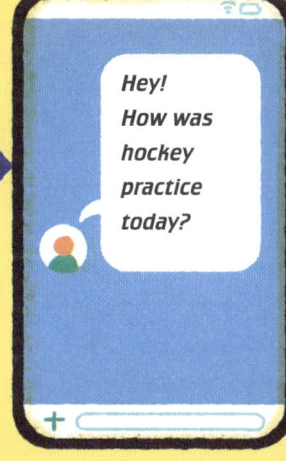

STEP 2. When you start a conversation with a friend, you both exchange your public keys.

STEP 3. Right before your message is sent, it's encrypted using your friend's public key. This encrypted message is sent through the internet, keeping the contents private. Even the makers of the messenger app won't be able to read it.

STEP 4. When your friend receives the message, their private key is used to decrypt it. Now they can see the message.

Breaking encryption

Unless you have the correct key, it's extremely difficult to decrypt a file. Someone might try a 'brute force attack', where a computer program tries to guess every possible key. But even superfast computers can take thousands of years to guess the right key.

When is something too secret?

Most of the time, encryption is used to protect our information, but there is a downside to this powerful technology. Criminals also use encrypted communications to hide what they are doing. Nonetheless, most people think this technology is still essential to protect regular citizens' private information.

PROTECTING YOUR PERSONAL DATA

When you buy something online, you need to tell the company your name and address so they know where to send the package. Often we need to share even more sensitive information – like our full names, date of birth or banking information. We rely on companies to protect that data and keep it safe. Yet, it's crucial as a responsible digital citizen to understand the risks.

Data breaches

When someone gets access to data they don't have permission to see, it is called a data breach. Most data breaches happen by mistake, such as accidentally giving the wrong people access. Other times, they happen on purpose, like when a cybercriminal tries to access certain data.

Companies have a responsibility to protect our personal data. There are different laws around the world that set out the rules on how it should be handled and stored. Companies can be fined or even put on trial if a data breach happens.

Mega metadata

Photos uploaded to the internet contain information about what time the photo was taken, the type of camera used and even the exact coordinates of where it was taken! This is called metadata. Most social media sites remove this sensitive data before an image is posted, but if you send a photo through a messenger app or email, the metadata could still be there. Anyone who had that photo could find out where it was taken and when, so be mindful of who you share your photos with.

DATA BLAST
THE RIGHT TO BE FORGOTTEN

You can email any company to ask them what information they hold about you and request they delete it – but some don't make it easy! Internet activists are campaigning to give people 'the right to be forgotten'. They want to make it easier for information about us to be deleted if it's wrong, out of date or just not relevant.

ON ASSIGNMENT
EVERY PHOTO TELLS A STORY

Sometimes we share our personal data by choice. People film vlogs, take photos and share what they are up to on social media. But oversharing your life can risk your safety. Look closely at this social media post. How might Jennifer be accidentally revealing personal information about her family? What are the risks of sharing this photo?

1. Can you spot the house number?

2. What's the registration plate number of their car?

3. Where is the family staying on holiday?

4. What is Dad's full name?

5. How long will they be away from home?

Finally! We're on our way to Mexico. Can't wait to spend 3 weeks relaxing in the sunshine!

Doxxing

Doxxing is when a person deliberately posts someone else's personal information on the internet. It could be their phone number, or details about where they live or go to school. You should never do this. It's cruel and distressing for the person involved and can put someone in danger. Even with your friends, remember to respect people's privacy and not share personal information about others.

DATA BLAST
GAMERTAGS

Never use your real name when playing games online. Instead, be like the pro gamers and call yourself by your 'gamertag'. You can show off your personality or interests without sharing private information.

COOL_G4M3B00

SOLVING BIG PROBLEMS

Is there intelligent life beyond Earth? How can we predict an earthquake before it happens? Can we find cures for diseases? Answering these big questions takes teamwork and technology. Here are some interesting ways the power of the internet is being used to tackle some of the world's trickiest challenges.

Searching for aliens from your living room

The Search for Extraterrestrial Intelligence project, or SETI@home, used internet tech to search for aliens. Researchers at the University of California, Berkeley, needed to scan through radio signals from space to see if any were messages from extraterrestrial life. They invited volunteers to help them... by downloading a screensaver!

When the screensaver activated, it processed a small chunk of the data, looking for patterns that might be alien signals. The results were sent back to a central server over the internet. By using the power of millions of computers, the project analysed more data than a single computer ever could.

While the project didn't find any alien signals, it proved people were willing to take part in online scientific experiments. Since then, more have cropped up. In Foldit, players solve puzzles by folding chains into different shapes. When they solve these puzzles, they're actually helping research into diseases. Tell that to someone who says you're wasting time playing games!

 **ON ASSIGNMENT**
GAMING ONLINE FOR GOOD

Want to play some internet games that help with scientific research? Search online for Phylo, NeMO-Net or Eyewire and get stuck in!

High-tech healthcare

Instead of travelling to different cities to treat patients, skilled surgeons can now perform operations over the internet. Robots carry out the surgery while being controlled remotely. Surgeons see what's happening through cameras and monitor important patient data on their computer screens. Some even use game controllers to operate!

The first remote surgery happened in 2001, when Professor Jacques Marescaux in New York, USA, performed gallbladder surgery on a patient in Strasbourg, France. Back then, they had to use special high-speed connections, not the internet, to make it work.

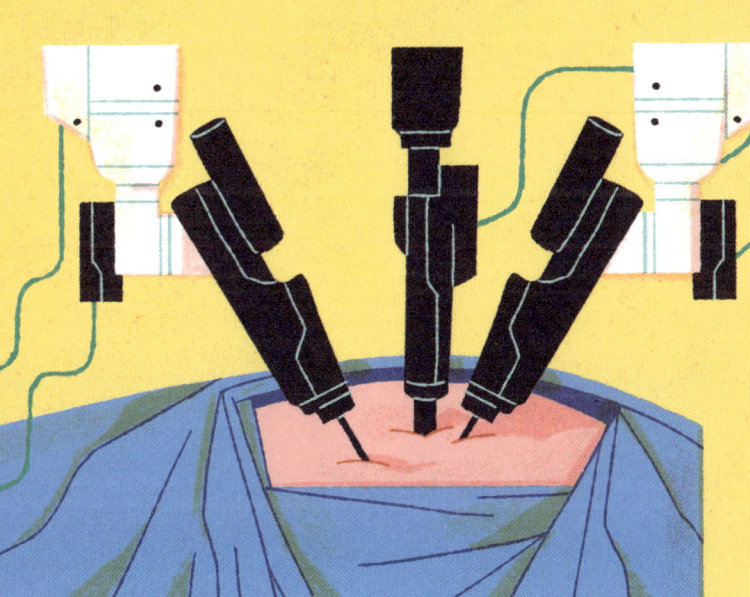

For these surgeries to be safe, the connection has to be super responsive so that when the surgeon moves, the robot mirrors that movement almost instantly. The internet wasn't fast enough for this previously, but with 5G internet connections responding in under one-thousandth of a second, remote surgery will become much more common.

Navigating natural disasters

When natural disasters strike, the sooner governments know about them, the more they can do to protect people. That's why countries are setting up early warning systems to detect them as quickly as possible. Early warning systems rely on sensors connected to the internet. These sensors send messages to each other and to a central computer to monitor for signs of danger. For example, water level sensors in rivers can alert if a river is about to overflow.

HOW THE INTERNET CHANGES LIVES

We've seen how the internet helps us work, play, learn and shop, but sometimes it lends a hand in the most unexpected ways. You never know when you might be just one click away from solving a mystery, bringing families together or even saving a life!

Rescued on camera!

Imagine being lost on a foggy, rain-soaked mountain in Alaska, USA. That's what happened to one unlucky hiker. Struggling to find his way to safety, he stumbled across a wildlife webcam that was streaming live! Thinking quickly, the hiker waved and signalled for help. Thankfully, fans watching the stream called the emergency services who rescued the man. It's not every day you get saved by a webcam!

Looking out for online friends

A teenage gamer in England was saved by his online friend over 8,000 kilometres away. Aidan had been playing games with Dia, who lived in Texas, USA. During their game, Aidan began to have a seizure and stopped responding. Dia acted fast and contacted UK emergency services for help. When the ambulance arrived, Aidan's parents had no idea anything was wrong. Thanks to the internet, Aidan was helped just in time.

Missing children found using social media

AS Roma, an Italian football club, launched an online campaign to help find missing children. When they announced new player signings on social media, they started including pictures of the children in their posts, which were viewed by millions of fans. Thanks to their posts, children from the UK, Kenya, Belgium, Poland and more have been reunited with their families.

Online fundraising

The internet can turn a small idea into something massive. Take the Ice Bucket Challenge, where people filmed themselves dumping ice-cold water over their heads to raise money for charity. It raised an astonishing $115 million for motor neurone disease research.

But you don't have to raise millions to make an impact. Isa, a teenager from Nottingham, UK, hosted a 'virtual sleep out'. He challenged teens to sleep in their gardens for a night to raise awareness about homelessness. Kids across the country used their home Wi-Fi to chat online and encourage each other throughout the night.

TikTok twins

Could the next TikTok video you watch change your life? For Amy and Ano, it did. The twin sisters from Georgia were separated at birth and neither twin knew the other existed. That all changed when Ano saw a TikTok of a girl that looked exactly like her. Determined to find her, Ano posted a plea in a WhatsApp group asking for help identifying the look-alike.

Ano used the internet to tap into a massive network and shared videos and photos, which really helped. Incredibly, a classmate knew Amy and connected the two, and finally, they found out they were long-lost twins!

HOW THE INTERNET CAN HARM US

The internet isn't always a fun place to be – it can take a dark turn. Sometimes, being online can mess with how we feel and even make us upset or sad. It's smart to know what things can impact our wellbeing online so we know how to deal with them and can keep things positive.

Cyber-bullying

Bullies can use the internet to harass and hurt people by sending threatening messages, making nasty comments or trying to isolate people from their friends and family. Online bullying feels easier because bullies can do it from a distance and hide behind accounts which disguise their identity. This lets them say and do things they would never do in person.

Action plan

Bullying is never okay. Here are some helpful ways to handle a bullying situation:

- **Don't respond** – never reply to a bully's messages, even if they make you angry.
- **Take a screenshot** – keep a record of what they've said.
- **Block the bully** – block and report them on the app or website they are using.
- **Tell an adult** – immediately tell someone you trust what's going on and show them what's been said or done.

Spotting unhealthy habits

Do you feel it's tough to focus on homework because apps keep pulling you in? They make every message seem so important that we feel like we have to check it straight away. But that's just a trick to keep us online. Ignore the notifications and focus on what matters, like spending time with friends and family.

Our internet habits can affect our physical wellbeing too. You could get sore eyes or a headache from too much screen time. Staying online late at night can also upset your sleeping pattern, leaving you tired and unfocussed the next day. With an adult, work together to take charge of your screen time and give your body and mind a break.

If it looks too good to be true…

People online can fool us by using AI-powered apps to create photos or videos that look totally real – even when they're not. A post might show jazzy trainers with built-in speakers that you can 'buy' (but they don't exist), or a scary news clip made to panic you. Your eyes can't spot these AI fakes, so ask yourself: is this post trying to play with my feelings so I tap without thinking? Check with a trusted website or an adult before you click or share.

DATA BLAST
CATFISH

A catfish is someone who tricks people by pretending to be someone else online. They might say they're a celebrity or just someone your age who's into the same hobbies. They use other people's photos and videos to look convincing.

HOW THE INTERNET IMPACTS THE ENVIRONMENT

Every time you go online, you're actually starting a chain of events. Your request gets sent to powerful servers in massive data centres. The thousands of servers in data centres work non-stop, and all this processing takes a lot of energy. With millions of computers connected to the internet, what does this mean for the environment?

Our internet impact

To keep data centres running, power stations burn fossil fuels, which releases carbon dioxide into the atmosphere, contributing to global warming and climate change. We add to this with our online actions.

Watching an hour of streaming video creates about 55 gCO_2e (grams of carbon dioxide equivalent) – the same as boiling an electric kettle three times.

Saving 1,000 photos in online storage for a year creates 1,000 gCO_2e – about the same as fully charging a smartphone 100 times.

Scrolling on social media for two hours creates about 165 gCO_2e – similar to driving a petrol car for a kilometre.

Making the internet greener

Data centres are finding ways to use less energy – they're getting better at keeping them cool and switching to energy-saving equipment that uses less power. Many have switched to solar or wind power. But as the internet keeps growing, we'll need to invent more ways to reduce the impact on the environment. Luckily engineers and scientists are always researching new greener technology to help protect the planet.

Commotion in the ocean

Undersea cables carry internet and power across the ocean, but laying them can cause disruption. When a cable is installed, it disturbs the seabed, which can destroy habitats nearby. Burying cables stirs up sediment, which can harm ocean animals.

These cables also create electromagnetic fields – areas around the cable that pull and push on electrical charges. Some marine animals rely on Earth's natural magnetic fields to navigate. Scientists are investigating whether these electromagnetic fields could interfere with their ability to do this.

Undersea cables don't release pollutants. When they're no longer needed, they can be recycled.

ASK ME ANYTHING

I'M REALLY CONCERNED ABOUT THE IMPACT OF THE INTERNET ON THE ENVIRONMENT. IS THERE ANYTHING I CAN DO?

Definitely! Keep your gadgets as long as possible – repair them instead of replacing them so they'll last longer. Recycle or donate old laptops and phones. Think about how you're using your tech – even little things like lowering your screen brightness help use less energy.

Precious minerals

One of the biggest environmental impacts of the internet comes from the production of computers, laptops and phones. Making these devices requires rare minerals like cobalt and lithium, which are needed for batteries and other electronic components. Gold is also used to connect parts of the circuit board.

Mining these materials uses lots of energy and water. Forests are cleared away to make way for mines, and machines create pollution. Also, since these minerals are found in very few places, high demand can lead to serious issues. In the Democratic Republic of the Congo, dangerous groups force people to work long hours in unsafe conditions and for very little money. Even children end up working in these mines and often miss school because of it.

CARING FOR THE INTERNET

Just like a plant, the internet needs care to grow and be healthy. But by looking after it, we can help it flourish into a place that's inspiring, knowledge-packed and inclusive of everyone. As users of the internet, we all play a part in looking after it – for ourselves and future generations.

Spread kindness in the comments

The internet can get pretty emotional. Some posts inspire us, but others make us upset and angry. It's easy to get riled up about things we see online, especially something we don't agree with or know is untrue. Some people's mean comments can spiral into the real world, making it harder for people to get along. Is that the kind of online world we want? By being respectful, kind and helpful when you post, you encourage others to do the same.

Turn your knowledge into resources

Everyone has something they can teach. Maybe you've written a guide to your favourite game, created a how-to video or put together a list of useful websites for a history project. Publish them online so others can benefit – it might be exactly what someone else is looking for!

Share your best shots

You've probably used someone else's photo in a school project before – why not give something back? If you have a photo that others would find useful, you can share it on sites like Wikimedia Commons or Unsplash, where you can give people permission to use your photos for free.

Make your photos accessible

When you share a photo online, you can add alternative text, or 'alt text' for short, to describe what's in the image. This helps people who are blind or have low vision to understand the image by allowing screen readers to read the description out loud. If you post a video, add closed captions to help people who are deaf or hard of hearing enjoy it too.

Be a helper online

Helping friends with their problems feels really rewarding, but did you know you can help out online too? You could give a hint to complete maths homework or reveal your secrets to baking the perfect cake. Just be sure to check with an adult before joining a new online community – they'll make sure it's a safe space.

Be a digital leader

Remember how exciting it was to go online for the first time? If you've got younger siblings, help them learn to use the internet safely. Show them your favourite apps and teach them how to search for information about things that interest them. You'll be helping make sure their first experiences of the internet are fun and friendly.

THE FUTURE OF THE INTERNET

Although it's come a long way already, the story of the internet is just beginning. It's amazing to imagine what the internet will look like 30 years from now. Think about how you use it today — what do you wish it could do that it can't yet? Let's look at what might be coming next!

Faster than ever before

Right now, one of the fastest ways to send data over the internet is through 5G radio waves. But even faster technology is already being researched! Telecommunications companies are working on 6G wireless connections that could be so quick, you could download an entire game in the blink of an eye!

Living near the edge

Instead of building more humongous data centres kilometres away from cities, there might be a shift to smaller 'edge' data centres built closer to where people live. With servers nearby, data travels a shorter distance, so websites load faster and video calls feel smoother.

Look up!

To reach places where cables can't, the solution might be in the sky! Engineers are testing solar-powered drones that hover 20 kilometres in the air and act like floating mobile towers. Along with the thousands of satellites expected to launch in the next decade, you'll soon see more internet infrastructure above you, rather than below the ground.

Internet you can wear

We already have smart glasses that connect to the internet, but could it go even further? What if your jacket told you to don your hood because the weather forecast predicted rain in the next five minutes? For some, the internet is already part of their wardrobe, with smartwatches and rings that go online. Now, it's becoming easier to add tiny computers, batteries and internet-capable chips directly into fabric.

Protecting our private data

In the future, the internet could be a place where we have full control over all our personal information. Imagine storing all your data in your own secure vault and deciding exactly who can open it. People are already working on building these systems, but the challenge is getting the companies that hold our information to use them.

Hugging from a distance

Over the years, the internet has gotten much better at making us feel like we're right there with someone, thanks to super clear video and audio. This is called telepresence, and it makes talking to people online feel more natural than ever! So, what's next?

Imagine special gloves or T-shirts that let you feel a hug or a handshake, thanks to tiny motors called actuators that make it feel real. How cool would it be to hug your grandparents from the other side of the world? Soon, using this type of tech could be as normal as sending a hug emoji.

WHAT'S YOUR INTERNET PERSONA?

There are lots of different personalities on the internet, but which one are you? Take this quiz to find out which of these internet personas is your closest match.

3. You find out that the internet in a nearby area is slow and expensive, making it hard for students to do their homework. What do you do?

A. Start a podcast sharing stories from students who struggle without fast internet.

B. Reach out to the council to ask for better Wi-Fi hotspots in libraries and community centres.

C. Start an online petition asking internet service providers to offer lower prices for students.

D. Build an app that uses less data so students with slow internet can access educational websites.

1. Your classmates need help promoting the school play. How do you lend a hand?

A. Film a vlog featuring interviews with the cast and share it on social media.

B. Create some flashy online targeted adverts to boost ticket sales.

C. Organise a fundraiser to buy props and costumes for the show.

D. Design a slick website with all the ticket information and an online booking form.

4. A cheeky squirrel that steals sips from smoothies has gone viral! How do you join in on the trend?

A. Record a dance – the 'squirrel shuffle' – and tag and challenge your followers to do the same.

B. Quickly set up an online shop and sell T-shirts you designed featuring the squirrel.

C. Write a blog post sharing fun squirrel facts and ways to protect local wildlife.

D. Code a game where players have to defend their smoothies from an army of smoothie squirrels.

2. You bought a new book online, then discovered the website has a bug that reveals customers' home addresses. You...

A. Message the bookseller on social media and warn your followers to avoid the website until it's fixed.

B. Report it and suggest to the bookseller that they offer you a discount for finding the bug.

C. Start an online campaign telling shops to better protect people's personal information.

D. Look through the website's code to spot the problem. Note your findings and send them to the bookseller's security team.

5. Your grandparents' home Wi-Fi is making video calls fuzzy and stutter. How would you help solve this problem?

A. Get clued up by watching tutorial videos, then record your own to share with your grandparents and followers.

B. Make a deal with their internet service provider to get the latest, most powerful router.

C. Take your grandparents to a local meet-up where volunteers give free tech support.

D. Run speed tests, adjust the router settings and find the best spot in the house to get a strong connection.

THE RESULTS!

MOSTLY As

You're a social media star. You know how to grab attention online and you're at your online best when you use your creativity to entertain, educate and bring people together!

MOSTLY Bs

You're an internet entrepreneur, always spotting opportunities to make deals and make money online. Thanks to your business sense, you always know what people want to spend their money on!

MOSTLY Cs

You're an internet activist who knows how to use the internet to stand up for causes you care about. You use your online voice to raise awareness about big issues.

MOSTLY Ds

You're a web wizard who loves playing with the latest gadgets and solving tricky problems. You create websites, apps and games for fun, keep the internet running smoothly, and help build our digital world!

SIGN OFF

Well done – you've made it to the end of our internet exploration! You've seen how from its early days, the internet has quickly changed our world. It's incredible to think about how far we've come in such a short time.

You now know about the cables that stretch the ocean floor, the data centres packed with powerful computers and the coding languages that make everything online possible. You've also learned about the skilled people who work to keep us connected, and you've read about the creatives and entrepreneurs who earn their living online, making videos, selling books or sharing their music and art.

Beyond that, I hope this book has opened your eyes to some of the internet's challenges. You've learned about its environmental impact, the dangers of cybercrime and how it can be used to spread misinformation. These are big issues, and perhaps you feel inspired to help make the internet a fairer and safer place. In the future, it might be your job to defend us against viruses and cyberattacks, or maybe you'll campaign to bring free internet access to those who need it. We need people like you to champion a better online world.

The internet is expanding each day and there's so much we didn't get the chance to investigate. As you grow up, you'll discover new ways to use the internet, like planning holidays or applying for jobs. But some things won't change – I still love using the internet to play games and chat with friends.

I hope now you understand how much I care about the internet. The internet is about connecting computers, but it's really about connecting all of us. I'm excited to see where it's headed and what new technologies will emerge.

To make it even better, we need more people like you to get involved – not just as users, but as makers and creators. Could that be you? Whatever you can imagine, you have the power to help build. Young innovators like you can shape the technology and lead the changes that make the internet better for everyone. Power on!

Logging off...

Craig Steele
Technologist, educator and author

GLOSSARY

Alternative (alt) text
A piece of text that describes a digital image, which is read aloud by screen reader software to help people understand what the image shows.

Artificial intelligence (AI)
A computer system built to solve problems or make decisions in ways that resemble human thinking. It works by spotting patterns in data and making predictions from them.

Bandwidth
The maximum amount of data that can travel through an internet connection each second, typically measured in megabits per second (Mbps).

Blog
An online journal where a person publishes posts about their life or interests using text, photos or videos.

Closed source
Source code for a piece of software which is kept secret, so it can only be looked at or changed by developers of the person or company who owns it.

Content
Anything available to read, watch, listen to or play online.

Cookies
Small files that are saved to your device to help a website keep track of your online activity. This helps websites to do things such as keep you logged in, remember what is in your basket or show you targeted adverts.

Creator
Someone who makes and shares content online for others to enjoy.

Data
Pieces of information that computers store and handle. Every file on a computer is made of data, and it can come in many forms, such as text, images, sound or video.

Data centre
A building filled with thousands of servers that store data for websites, apps and online games, and receive and send data to computers around the world.

Decentralisation
A way to describe how internet data is stored on thousands of computers around the world instead of on one central server. This also means that no single person can control it, make decisions about it or turn it off.

E-commerce
Buying or selling over the internet through online shops or marketplaces.

Email
Short for 'electronic mail'. Digital letters sent across the internet.

Encryption
A method of scrambling data so that it can't be read without a special digital key to unlock it.

Influencer
A person with a large online following whose opinions and reviews shape what their fans think or buy.

Internet of Things (IoT)
Everyday objects that have the ability to connect to the internet to share data or be controlled remotely, such as lights, watches, televisions and even cars.

Internet service provider (ISP)
A company that provides the service of connecting homes, public services and businesses to the internet.

IP address
A string of numbers that identify your device on the internet. An IP address might look like 192.0.2.0.

Mobile network
A web of cell towers and antennas that lets phones make calls, send texts and access the internet wirelessly while on the move.

Mobile network operator
A company that builds and runs a mobile network and sells packages called data plans, which allow people and companies to access that network.

Modem
A device that converts the internet signal from an internet service provider into data that home devices can understand. Today, modems are often built into home Wi-Fi routers.

Net neutrality
The idea that internet service providers should treat all online data equally, without speeding up, slowing down or blocking websites unfairly.

Open source
Source code for a piece of software that is shared, so that anyone can read it, improve it or remix it.

Overconsumption
Buying or using far more items and things than a person really needs or can realistically use, which wastes resources and energy. This could be clothes and food, but also digital content like video or music streams.

Personal data
Information that can be used to identify you, such as your name, your address, photos of yourself, health records and banking details.

Programming languages
Languages to write instructions (called code) that a computer follows. Different languages are used for different tasks.

Router
A device that directs data to the right place on a network. At home, your router creates the Wi-Fi and links gadgets to the internet. In data centres, high-speed routers do the same job for data travelling across countries and continents.

Server
A powerful computer that stores the data for websites and apps and sends requested data to other devices. Millions of servers around the world work together to host the internet.

Social media
Websites and apps where people can create profiles, share posts and communicate with other people.

Software
A set of computer programs and applications that instruct a computer or device to perform a specific task. For example, a web browser is software that lets you visit websites.

Source code
Instructions written in a computer programming language that a computer can run. Source code can be read by a human.

Streaming
Playing audio or video files over the internet instead of a file you have downloaded.

Targeted advertising
Advertisements that are chosen specially for a certain audience based on data such as someone's search history, location or likes.

Throttling
When an internet service provider or mobile network operator deliberately slows your internet speed.

URL
Stands for 'Uniform Resource Locator'. This is the address you type to visit a website.

Vlog
Short for 'video blog', this is when a creator – sometimes called a vlogger – films a video talking to the camera about their life, hobbies and interests, and posts it online.

Web app
Software or an application that you visit in a web browser and use online, instead of installing a separate program on your device.

Website
A collection of web pages, images and files stored on a server, accessed on the internet. All the parts of a website share the same main URL.

Wi-Fi
Wireless technology that connects us to the internet. Wi-Fi uses radio waves to link your devices to a router, which then connects them to the internet.